PLANT LIFE

Peter Riley

Franklin Watts®
A Division of Scholastic Inc.
New York   Toronto   London   Auckland   Sydney
Mexico City   New Delhi   Hong Kong
Danbury, Connecticut

Picture credits:
Cover : Holt Studios Internationals
(N. Cattlin); Bruce Coleman pp. 5b
(H. Reinhard), 10t (Dr. E. Pott), 16b
(E. Crichton), 29t (T. Buchholz);
Garden Picture Library pp. 4l
(J. Glover), 12t (R. Sutherland); Frank
Lane Picture Agency pp. 5m
(H. Clark), 6 (W. Broadhurst), 9t
(M. Nimmo), 14b (Life Science
Images), 18b (R.P. Lawrence), 26t
(G.E. Hyde); Holt Studios
International pp.14t (N. Cattlin), 23r
(N. Cattlin), 24b (N. Cattlin), 29b
(N. Cattlin); Natural History
Photographic Agency PP. 5t (G.J.
Cambridge), 8t (M.I. Walker), 19r
(S. Dalton); Oxford Scientific Films
pp. 8b (H. Taylor), 9b (H. Taylor), 11t
(C. Milkins), 13bl (G.I. Bernard), 15t
(London Scientific Films), 18t
(Animals Animals/ Breck P. Kent),
19l (M. Leach), 20m (D. Wright), 22t
(H. Taylor), 22b (G.I. Bernard), 23l
(London Scientific Films), 26b
(H. Taylor), 27t (G.A. Maclean), 27m
(G.I. Bernard), 27b (R. Day);
Derek Whitford p. 13tl.

Series editor: Sarah Snashall
Designer: Mo Choy
Picture research: Sue Mennell
Photography: Steve Shott
(unless otherwise credited)
Artwork: Peter Bull

First published in 1998 by
Franklin Watts

First American edition 1999 by
Franklin Watts
An Imprint of Scholastic Inc.
557 Broadway
New York, NY 10012

A CIP catalog record for this
book is available from the
Library of Congress.

ISBN 0-531-14507-7 (lib.bdg)
ISBN 0-531-15373-8 (pbk)

© Franklin Watts 1998
Text © Peter Riley 1998

Printed in China, Dongguan
November 2009
PO100244

CONTENTS

A WORLD OF PLANTS

There are thousands of different kinds of plant. They can be found in most places on Earth. Some tiny plants float in the sunlit waters of seas and lakes. Others live on the sea shore but most live on land.

WHAT IS A PLANT?

A plant is a living thing that uses the energy in sunlight to make its own food. Plants have many different features. Some plants have a root to secure them to a certain place in the ground. Some have a shoot made up of a stem, leaves, and sometimes flowers. Some plants reproduce by making seeds, other plants make spores. Spores and seeds grow into new plants. We use these features to put plants into groups.

Conifer leaves are thin and waxy and grow all year round.

FLOWERING PLANTS

Flowering plants are the most common type of plant. They have roots, stems, leaves, and flowers. The flowers make seeds.

Many flowering plants can be grown in pots.

CONIFERS

Conifers are trees. They have roots and a shoot with a stem and leaves. Most conifers breed by making seeds in cones. The largest living thing on Earth is a conifer tree called a Giant Sequoia.

FERNS

Ferns have roots, stems, and large leaves called fronds. On the underside of the frond are dark lumps which release spores into the air.

Many ferns grow in shady places in woods.

ALGAE

Algae do not have stems, leaves, or roots. They live in water or on damp surfaces of rocks and breed by producing spores. Most algae are so small that they can only be seen with a microscope. Some live together in colonies which can be seen as a green patch.

The largest type of algae are the sea weeds.

MOSSES

Mosses have stems and leaves but they do not have proper roots. They grow on rocks, tree stumps, and on the surface of the soil. When moss plants breed, a stalk with a swollen tip called a capsule grows above the leaves. The capsule releases spores which are carried away by the air currents.

Moss plants are only a few inches high.

FLOWERING PLANTS

The body of a flowering plant is divided into two parts. They are the root and the shoot. The root grows in the ground and the shoot grows above it in the air or along the ground.

ROOTS

The roots hold the plant in the ground. They stop it from being blown away by a strong wind or from being pulled out of the soil by an animal.

The root takes up water from the soil. Each root has tiny hairs along part of its length. They grow out between the soil particles and collect water covering their surfaces. When the roots take up water, they also take up minerals that are dissolved in the water. The minerals are chemicals that help the plant to grow.

This tree is held in the bank by its strong roots.

THE SHOOT

The shoot is made up of a stem, leaves, buds, and flowers. There is a large bud at the tip of the shoot and smaller buds down its sides. The shoot increases its length when the bud at the tip bursts open. A stem with leaves and one or more flowers grows out of the bud.

When the side buds burst open, they form side shoots with leaves and flowers. A side bud grows just above the place where a leaf sprouts from the stem.

This branch of an apple tree grew from a bud. More side shoots are growing out of the branch.

■ INVESTIGATE!

Look at a shoot and find the buds next to the leaves.
Examine the way buds and leaves are arranged along the shoot.

A Closer Look at Plants

If you look at a piece of a plant under a microscope, you will see that it is made of tiny "boxes". Each "box" is called a cell. There are different kinds of cell in a plant. Each kind of cell has a special task in keeping the plant alive.

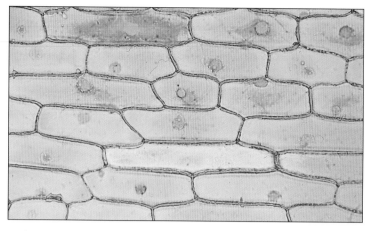

The oval nuclei in the cells of this onion skin can be seen clearly.

The Control Center of a Cell

In the cell is a spot of material called a nucleus. It controls the activities of the cell and keeps it alive.

Cells that Support the Stem

The center of the stem is filled with large cells. The cells hold water and this makes the stem firm so that the leaves can spread out to catch light from the sun. If the cells do not have enough water, the stem collapses and we say that the plant has wilted.

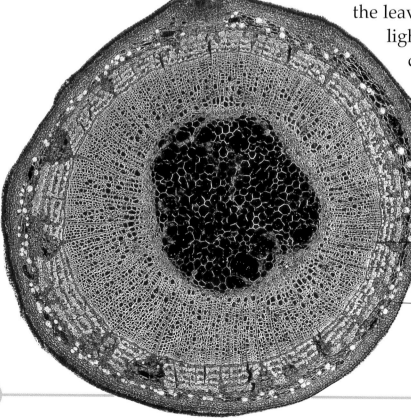

The different kinds of cells inside a stem.

cells which make the water-carrying tubes

cells which form the food-carrying tubes

TUBES IN THE PLANT

Some cells join together
to make tubes. Some of the tubes
carry water up from the root to the leaves
on the shoot. They have strong walls which
also help to hold up the shoot. Another set
of tubes carry food made in the leaves to
other parts of the plant.

*The tubes which carry
water in tree trunks are arranged
in a ring. Each year the stem
grows a new ring of tubes.*

■ INVESTIGATE!

The stringy threads in a celery stalk
are groups of tubes that carry water.
Put some ink in a glass of water and
stand a celery stalk in it. After half an
hour, see how far the ink has gone up
the tubes in the stalk.

*The cells in this stem have joined
together to form tubes.*

How Plants Make Food

Plants use the energy in the sunlight to turn water, carbon dioxide, and minerals into food. This process of using light to make food is called photosynthesis.

Trapping Energy
A green plant makes most of its food in its leaves. The cells in the leaf contain small disks called chloroplasts which are filled with a green pigment called chlorophyll. The chlorophyll absorbs energy from sunlight.

The Leaf's Water Supply
The plant needs water, and minerals dissolved in water, to photosynthesize. The plant draws water and minerals from the soil in through its roots. The water flows upward through the tiny tubes in the root and shoot.

Some water escapes through holes in the leaves called stomata. This causes more water to be pulled up through the roots.

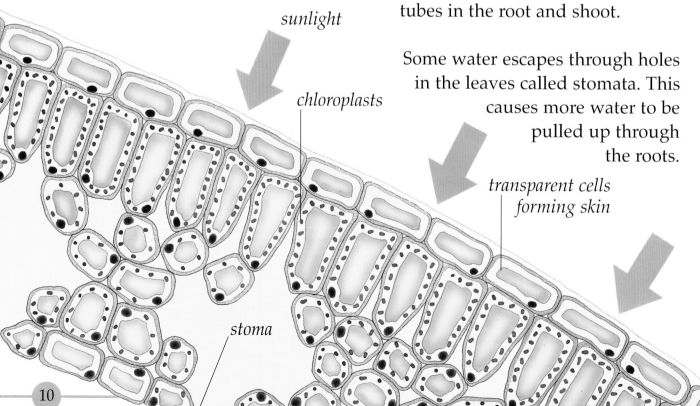

sunlight

chloroplasts

transparent cells forming skin

stoma

GREEN PLANTS AND AIR

The leaf takes in a gas from the air called carbon dioxide. The energy from sunlight is used to change the carbon dioxide and water into a food called carbohydrate and a gas called oxygen. The oxygen passes out of the leaf into the air.

Bubbles of oxygen have left this water plant after photosynthesis.

 water
food

The food made in the leaves is transported to other parts of the plant by tiny tubes in the shoot.

■ INVESTIGATE!

Cut a hole in the side of a cardboard box and put it over a pot of seedlings. Leave it for a few days then see how the seedlings have grown to the light passing through the hole.

THE PARTS OF A FLOWER

A plant can make its own food, but it needs help to reproduce. Flowering plants make a substance called pollen in their flowers. The pollen has to be moved from one part of a flower to another part. This process is called pollination.

INSECT-POLLINATED PLANTS

Insect-pollinated plants use insects to carry the pollen from one flower to another. They attract insects to the flower with bright petals and sweet nectar.

Petals

The sepals protected the flower when it was a bud.

The stigma receives pollen.

Style

Stamens. The swollen tip is called an anther. It makes pollen.

The ovary contains smaller structures called ovules. Each ovule can produce a seed.

At the base of the flower are nectaries that make nectar.

florets

FLORETS

Some plants make many small flowers called florets which form a group called a flower head like this gerbera.

carpels

CARPELS

Some flowers, such as the celandine, do not have an ovary. Instead, they have a number of small structures called carpels. Each one contains an ovule which can become a seed.

WIND-POLLINATED FLOWERS

Wind-pollinated flowers use the wind to blow pollen from one flower to another.

These flowers do not have petals or nectaries, but they do have stamens and an ovary. The stamens have long stalks and hang outside the flower so the wind can blow away the pollen. The stigma also hangs outside the flower to catch pollen floating in the wind.

Grass flowers grow together at the top of a stalk. These have hung out their anthers to release their pollen.

POLLINATION

A grain of pollen contains a nucleus of a cell. This nucleus has to reach the stigma of a flower to help the plant reproduce. Pollination is the process in which the pollen moves from an anther to a stigma.

A bee picks up pollen as it brushes past the anthers to feed on the nectar.

INSECT POLLINATION

Most flowers are pollinated by insects. The insects are attracted to the flowers to feed. The pollen grains of insect-pollinated flowers have spikes covering their surfaces. When an insect such as a bee visits a flower with ripe anthers, the pollen spikes stick to the hairs on the bee's body.

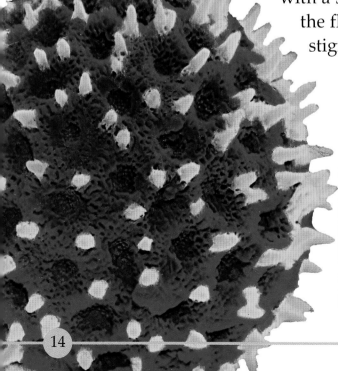

The pollen stays on the bee until it reaches a flower with a sticky stigma. As the bee goes down into the flower to feed on the nectar the sticky stigma pulls the pollen off the bee's hairs.

The spikes on the pollen's surface make it cling to the insect's hairs as the insect flies between flowers.

INVESTIGATE!

Look at the flowers of plants around your home or school. Find the stigma and the anthers.

WIND POLLINATION

The pollen from wind-pollinated flowers is very light in weight so that it can be carried away by very gentle winds. Large amounts of pollen are produced to increase the chance of some reaching another flower.

The pollen is released into the air by the anther of one flower and is caught by the stigma from another flower. The stigmas on wind-pollinated flowers have many fine strands like a feather which form a net to catch pollen blowing by.

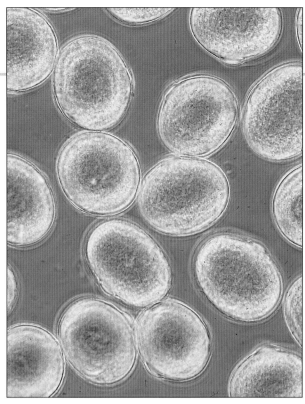

The pollen of wind-pollinated flowers have smooth surfaces because they do not need to grip onto an animal's body.

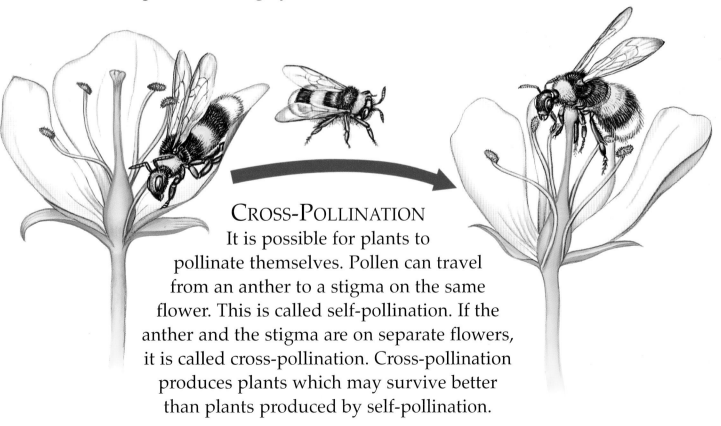

CROSS-POLLINATION

It is possible for plants to pollinate themselves. Pollen can travel from an anther to a stigma on the same flower. This is called self-pollination. If the anther and the stigma are on separate flowers, it is called cross-pollination. Cross-pollination produces plants which may survive better than plants produced by self-pollination.

How a Seed Is Made

After pollination, the nucleus in the pollen grain must reach a nucleus in an ovule. Once this has happened, an ovule can become a seed.

FERTILIZATION

When a pollen grain lands on a stigma, a tube grows out of its side. The pollen tube grows down through the stigma and style and into an ovule in the ovary.

The nucleus in the pollen grain moves along the tube and enters the ovule. Here, it joins with another nucleus. The joining of one nucleus with another in this way is called fertilization. Fertilization changes the ovule into a seed.

pollen grains on stigma

style

pollen tube

ovule

LOTS OF SEEDS

There may be many pollen grains which land on a stigma. Each one can fertilize an ovule. If there are many ovules in the ovary, fertilization may form many seeds.

Each of these peas has formed from a separate pollen grain and ovule. The ovary has become the pod.

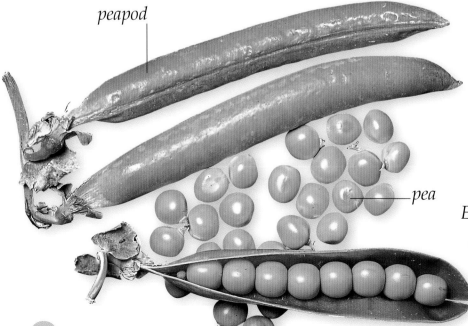

peapod

pea

CHANGES IN THE FLOWER

After fertilization has taken place, the flower is no longer needed and its petals and stamens dry up and fall off. The ovary changes its shape and color and becomes a fruit. Some fruits like the tomato take in water and form a fleshy wall around the seeds.

Remains of the flower

The kiwi fruit, avocado, orange, and tomato are all fruits with fleshy walls.

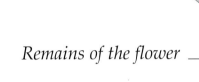

INVESTIGATE!

The tomato is a fruit. Cut a tomato open and see how the seeds are arranged inside it. How many seeds are there in a tomato?

# FRUITS

A fruit forms from an ovary. It contains one or more seeds and it helps them to spread out, or disperse, from the parent plant. Seeds need to spread out, so that the plants that grow from them do not compete with each other for space, water, and light.

FRUITS AND ANIMALS

Some fruits can be dispersed by sticking to animals. They have hooks and spines that stick to fur and feathers. Mammals and birds pick them up on their bodies as they brush against the parent plant. The fruits may be carried many miles before they drop off.

This burdock fruit will travel far from the parent plant on this dog's fur.

The seeds from many fruits are dispersed by passing through the body of an animal. These seeds develop in fruits which produce a soft, tasty substance around the seeds to attract animals. When the animal eats the fruit, it swallows the seeds. The seeds leave the animal in its droppings far from the parent plant.

This mouse swallows blackberry seeds and fruit. The seeds will be dispersed in the mouse's droppings.

A gust of wind can push so strongly on the dandelion fruits that they break free and scatter.

FRUIT IN THE AIR

Fruits which use the air to carry them grow special parts to increase their air resistance. This makes the fruit and the seed fall more slowly and be carried farther on the wind. Some fruits, like the maple, have wings, while fruits like the dandelion have a tuft of hairs, these act as a parachute.

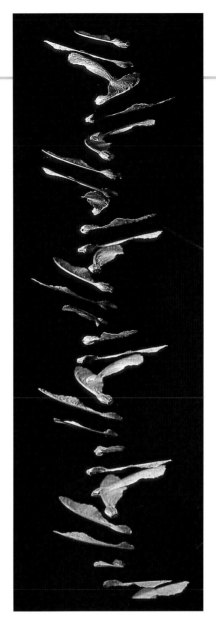

These sycamore fruits spin like helicopter rotors.

▐ INVESTIGATE!

Make a model of a winged fruit from a piece of paper 2 in (6 cm) long and 1½ in (4 cm) wide. Screw up about ¾ in (2 cm) of one end of the paper and tear the other end to make two wings ¾ in (2 cm) wide. Drop your fruit and watch it spin. How does changing the size of the wings change the way the model fruit spins?

SEEDS

A seed is a capsule that contains a tiny plant and a store of food to help the plant grow. Flowering plants and conifers reproduce by making seeds. A seed may be as small as a speck of dust or as large as a coconut, but all seeds have similar parts.

There is a great range in the size and shape of seeds.

The insect is unable to get through the strong coat of this acorn.

THE SEED COAT

The tiny plant and its food store are covered by a seed coat. This forms a hard surface which prevents many kinds of insects from biting their way into the seed and feeding on its contents.

The scar on the seed coat of this broad bean shows where it was attached to the ovary.

INSIDE A SEED

In many seeds, such as the broad bean seed, there are two large food stores. Between them is one tiny plant called an embryo plant. It looks a little like a walking stick. The "handle" is the tiny shoot and the straight part of the "stick" is the tiny root. Each food store is connected to the embryo plant by a short stalk.

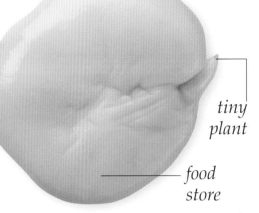

tiny plant

food store

WHY SEEDS ARE DRY

Before the seed leaves the plant, most of the water it contains is removed. This stops the seed from growing mold. The seed coat prevents water from entering the seed and it remains unharmed in the soil until it is time for the tiny plant to grow.

■ INVESTIGATE!

The appearance, size, and weight of a seed changes as it takes in water. Put some dry pea seeds or bean seeds in water for a day and see how they change.

SEEDS IN THE SOIL

Some seeds may stay in the soil for many years without taking in water. They are said to be dormant. The seed will stay dormant in the soil until the conditions are right for it to grow.

GERMINATION

The shoots of these coconut seedlings have grown out after the roots have grown into the sand.

When the conditions are right, the tiny embryo plant inside the seed takes in water and begins to grow. We say the seed germinates.

WHY SEEDS NEED WATER

In the dormant seed, the cells of the embryo plant are resting and little water is needed for them.

When the embryo plant begins to grow, new cells are produced which need water to keep them alive so more water is taken into the seed. The water also lets the food move from the food stores to the embryo plant to help it to grow.

WHEN THE ROOT GROWS

The part of the embryo plant to grow first is the root. It bursts out of the seed coat and grows down into the soil. Water passes into the plant through the surface of the root. Hairs grow out of the root to increase the surface for taking up water so that plenty of water can be taken in for the rapidly-growing plant.

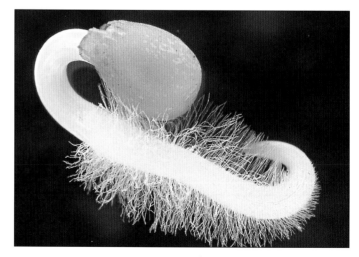

The root of this mustard seed grows out through the broken seed coat and sprouts hairs to collect water from the soil.

THE FIRST SHOOT

There are two ways in which the shoot of the embryo plant may grow. In some plants, such as peas and beans, the shoot may grow out from between the food stores and push upward through the soil and into the air.

In plants like the sunflower the shoot takes the food stores with it as it grows through the soil. When the shoot reaches the air the food stores turn green and become the first leaves.

In both kinds of plant, when the plant has grown a shoot and leaves it is called a seedling. The seedling can make its own food.

The leaves on this sunflower seedling are formed from the food stores which were inside the seed.

The broad bean shoot leaves the food stores behind as it grows upward.

MAKING IDENTICAL PLANTS

Some flowering plants also use a second method of reproducing. They make small copies of themselves. In time these new plants grow up to be identical to the parent plant.

This strawberry plant has put out a runner to produce a new plant.

GROWING OFF A STALK

The strawberry plant sends out side shoots with buds called runners. When each bud opens it forms a small plant. At first, the leaves get the water they need through the runner from the parent plant's roots. Soon the new plant grows roots to collect its own water from the soil and the runner, which is no longer needed, withers away.

POTATO TUBERS

New potato plants grow from swellings called tubers. The tubers, which we call potatoes, grow on underground side shoots. When the potato plant dies, the potatoes remain in the soil. The following year, each potato becomes a new potato plant.

This potato plant has made ten tubers.

This bud is growing into a bulb.

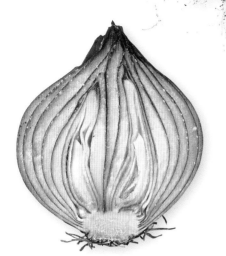

Two new shoots are forming inside this onion bulb.

MAKING NEW BULBS

Some plants like the tulip form a bulb. The bulb is made from parts of leaves that are swollen with food. The leaves that made the food have died away. Some of the food the leaves made is sent into buds on the stem. The buds swell up to form new bulbs. When the bulbs separate they form a group or clump of plants.

■ INVESTIGATE!

The spider plant is a house plant grown in many homes which produces runners. Cut some small spider plants from their runners. Plant them in soil and see how they grow.

TAKING A CUTTING

A clone of some plants, such as the geranium, can be made by cutting off a leaf or a side shoot and placing it in water or damp soil. The leaf or shoot grows roots and can be grown into a new plant.

THE LIFE CYCLE OF PLANTS

A plant's growth from seed to fully grown plant that reproduces is called its life cycle. Some plants have a life cycle which is over in a few weeks while others may live for hundreds of years.

A SHORT LIFE CYCLE

Some plants have a life cycle that is only a few weeks. These plants are called ephemerals. The seeds of ephemerals germinate soon after they are dispersed so that the life cycle of one plant can follow another through the spring to the autumn.

The Shepherd's Purse, above, is an ephemeral plant.

ONE YEAR LIFE CYCLE

Many plants complete their life cycle in one year. They are called annual plants. Their seeds are usually formed and dispersed in the autumn by the parent plants. During the winter the seeds survive in the soil and in the following spring they germinate. The seedlings grow up during the spring and the plants become full grown by the summer and produce flowers. Fruits are formed in the late summer which contain seeds for the following year. When the seeds are dispersed the plants die.

The marigolds and petunias in this flower bed are annuals.

TWO YEAR LIFE CYCLE

Plants which have a two year life cycle are called biennials. The carrot is a biennial and at the end of its first year it stores food in its root so it can use it in the following to help it grow flowers and produce seeds.

LONG-LIVED PLANTS

Plants which live for many years are called perennials. Parts of the shoot of perennial plants may die away at the end of the growing season while other parts of the shoot and the roots live on underground.

Woody flowering plants such as trees and bushes are perennials but their shoots do not die back. Their leaves fall off and the shoot is protected from the winter weather by the bark.

These carrots are being dug up to provide food for people instead of letting them grow shoots again next year.

The iris is a perennial. After its leaves die away its underground shoot and roots live in the soil through the winter.

The bark insulates these tree trunks from the cold weather.

GROWING PLANTS

Plants provide our food. Most of our meals contain parts of plants. Even meat comes from animals that have eaten plants. As the number of people on the planet continues to get larger, more and more food is needed. This can be provided by making crop plants grow as well as possible.

The parts of many different plants are good to eat.

ADDING MINERALS

Minerals are chemicals in the soil that plants need for healthy growth. In natural habitats, such as woodlands, the minerals the plants take from the soil passes back into the soil again when the plant dies. When crop plants are grown, they are taken away to be eaten and the amount of minerals in the soil falls. Manure from animals, or fertilizers made in the chemical industry, are spread on the soil to put the minerals back.

PESTICIDES

The growth of a plant can be slowed down by insects or fungi growing on it, or by weeds taking the minerals from the soil around it. The insects, fungi, and weeds are called pests, and to get rid of pests, farmers treat crops with pesticides. Pesticides are chemicals that kill the pests but leave the crops unharmed.

Spraying pesticides keeps the crop growing well.

INVESTIGATE!

Germinate seeds in two plant pots and when the seedlings start growing cover one of the pots with an upturned transparent jar. Compare how the two pots of seedlings grow on a sunny windowsill.

GREENHOUSES

A greenhouse traps heat energy from the sun inside it and this warms the air, soil, and plants. The warmth makes the plants grow faster. It also keeps the plants growing when it is too cold for them to survive outside.

These plants are thriving in the warm sunny greenhouse.

GLOSSARY

ALGAE—green plants without flowers that are mainly very small and live in water

ANTHER—the part of the flower that makes pollen

BUD—a structure on the shoot from which side shoots, leaves, and flowers may grow

CAPSULE—a container

CELL—a tiny living structure. The bodies of plants and animals are made up from large numbers of cells

CHLOROPHYLL—a green substance found in leaves that absorbs some of the energy in sunlight

CHLOROPLAST—a structure in a plant cell that contains chlorophyll

CLONE—a plant or an animal that is identical to its parent

CONIFER—a woody plant with needle-like leaves that bears cones instead of flowers. Most conifers make their seeds in the cones

CROP—a plant grown to provide food for people or animals

CROSS-POLLINATION—the transfer of pollen from the flower of one plant to the flower of another plant of the same kind

FERN—a non-flowering plant that has large feather-like leaves called fronds

FERTILIZATION—the process in which the nucleus from the pollen joins with a nucleus in the ovule to make a seed

FERTILIZER—a substance which is made from chemicals that contains the minerals a plant needs for growth

FLOWERING PLANT—a plant with root, stem, and leaves that reproduces by means of flowers

GERMINATION—the process in which a seed breaks open and the plant it contains begins to grow

HABITAT—a place such as a woodland or a pond where plants and animals live

LEAF—a structure on a plant that makes food

MANURE—the droppings of animals that are spread on the soil to give it extra minerals

MINERALS—chemicals in the soil that the plant needs for healthy growth

MOSS—small plants with stems and leaves but without proper roots

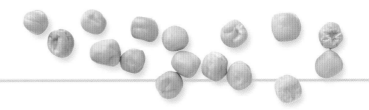

NECTAR—a liquid containing sugar that provides food to insects visiting flowers

NECTARY—a structure at the bottom of a flower that produces nectar

NUCLEUS—the structure in a cell that controls the cell's activities

OVARY—a part of the flower that contains the ovules. After fertilization, it forms the fruit which contains the seeds

OVULE—a structure inside the ovary which becomes a seed once it has been fertilized

PETAL—the part of the flower that attracts insects to it by its color

POLLEN—tiny grains made by the anther of a flower. Each grain contains a nucleus

POLLINATION—the transfer of pollen from an anther to a stigma

REPRODUCE—to make new individuals such as the young in animals or seedlings in plants

ROOT—the part of the plant that grows underground. It holds the plant in the ground and collects water and minerals for it to make food

SEED—a structure that contains a tiny plant and its food store

SELF-POLLINATION—the transfer of pollen from the anther of a flower to its stigma or to the stigma of another flower on the same plant

SHOOT—the part of the flowering plant above the ground that includes the stem, branches, leaves, and flowers

SPORE—a tiny structure that contains part of a non-flowering plant such as a moss or a fern and travels in the air, settles on the ground, and grows into a new plant

STAMEN—the part of the flower that is made up of the anther and the stalk that supports it

STEM—the part of the shoot that supports branches, leaves, and flowers

STIGMA—the part of the flower that receives the pollen grains

STYLE—the stalk that connects the stigma to the ovary

INDEX